YOUR KNOWLEDGE HAS VALUE

Derya Heper

Aus der Reihe: e-fellows.net stipendiaten-wissen

e-fellows.net (Hrsg.)

Band 981

Can we improve the situation of the Russian Timber Industry?

GRIN Verlag

Bibliografische Information der Deutschen Nationalbibliothek:

Die Deutsche Bibliothek verzeichnet diese Publikation in der Deutschen National-
bibliografie; detaillierte bibliografische Daten sind im Internet über http://dnb.d-
nb.de/ abrufbar.

Imprint:

Copyright © 2012 GRIN Verlag GmbH
Druck und Bindung: Books on Demand GmbH, Norderstedt Germany
ISBN: 978-3-656-73466-6

This book at GRIN:

http://www.grin.com/en/e-book/279567/can-we-improve-the-situation-of-the-russian-
timber-industry

GRIN - Your knowledge has value

Der GRIN Verlag publiziert seit 1998 wissenschaftliche Arbeiten von Studenten, Hochschullehrern und anderen Akademikern als eBook und gedrucktes Buch. Die Verlagswebsite www.grin.com ist die ideale Plattform zur Veröffentlichung von Hausarbeiten, Abschlussarbeiten, wissenschaftlichen Aufsätzen, Dissertationen und Fachbüchern.

Seminar Course

Documentation

Russia

Continuity And Change

Can we improve the situation of

the Russian timber industry?

Derya Heper J1a

Königin-Olga-Stift

25 May 2012

Table of Contents

1. Introduction

"The forests are carrying the heaven. If we are cutting them, disasters will follow." That is a common legend from the Indians.[1]

We are cutting the forests, so it is interesting to look at the problems resulting from this. The general topic is Russia, and actually the Russian timber industry has to suffer from different problems. In this documentation I will answer the question "Can we improve the situation of the Russian timber industry?"

The Russian timber industry means the forests in Russia, the exporting wood and also all processed timber products exported to other countries. The situation of this economic sector is not optimal at the moment, but the conditions are quite good, so there is hope. If we get solutions for the main problems, it is possible to solve them in the future.

At first I will treat forestry in general and the Russian industry in general, so that the Russian timber industry is understandable and in a context. Then I will talk about the situation of the Russian timber industry in general because this knowledge is necessary to understand the problems. After that I will illustrate the resulting problems the Russian timber industry has today. The first one will be the economic problems. The next problem is illegal logging, which leads to many other problems. Other problems I will deal with are the environmental difficulties like the burnings of the forest. After knowing all this I will give some possible solutions. In the end I will give a conclusion, which functions like a short summary.

This topic fits very well in the general topic of our Seminar Course because the Russian timber industry is very important. Russia exports the largest amount of timber all over the world, so it is interesting to have a closer look at this economic sector. Like in many other fields in Russia, there is also continuity in the timber industry because many problems are still the same, like wildfires and illegal logging. But there are also many aspects which have changed in the last years. The economy is permanently changing. In nearly each chapter you will recognise the change and the continuity of each problem.

---

[1] Launer, Ekkehard: *Zum Beispiel Holz. Hört mit der Zerstörung der Wälder auf, oder wir sind gezwungen, sie zu verteidigen.* Göttingen: Lamuv Verlag: 1989 : page 31

2. Forestry in general

Before we can start talking about the Russian timber industry we have to look at the forestry in general to have a general overview.

For most of the people, in the Ancient Times, the middle Ages and today, the forest is a place of recreation and recovery. It was also used like that although the importance and the usage of forests changed during the centuries. [2]

When we are talking about the timber industry at first we have to define the most important terms, which are forest and cultivated forest.

Forest means an area where many trees are growing. The forest belongs to the originally forms of vegetation which proceed all kinds of human culture. This type we call primeval forest.[3]

Cultivated forest is a forest which is established for a regular economical enterprise.[4]

The difference between this two is that a cultivated forest is used to make profits and for economic aims.

Since the 18th century regional and international timber markets were developing in Europe. A lot of money was earned in this sector. This earned money was partly used to pay the protection and creation of the forests.[5] Back in the past forest was a treasure and the owner got very rich. But for a couple of years the income of timber sells does not cover the costs of the business anymore. Therefore new solutions are necessary. On top of that the protection of the environment must be regarded, too. [6]

Generally you can say that the forestry sector has to face more and more problems in the whole world because the forest areas are getting less and natural disasters are increasing a lot. It needed a hundred million years to create the rainforest. It needed 40 years for the human beings to destroy half of it. So if we do not act now, there will be no

---

[2] Holzberger, Rudi / Fesseler, Ernst: *Der Wald. Zwischen Wildnis und Monokultur*. Ravensburg: Buchverlag Otto Maier 1989: page 86
[3] Köpf, Ernst Ulrich: *Forstpolitik*. Stuttgart: Verlag Eugen Ulmer 2002: page 68
[4] Ibid: page 68
[5] Zundel, Rolf: *Einführung in die Forstwirtschaft*. Stuttgart: Verlag Eugen Ulmer 1990: page 69-70
[6] Köpf, Ernst Ulrich: page 68

rainforest in 40 years anymore.[7] But not only the rainforests are concerned, the protection of the forest and nature are also important in Europe and Asia.

3. The Russian industry in general

Russia wants to become more important in the world market. In this case Russia is very ambitious.[8] Russia wants to be separated from the other states, but in the same moment it does not want to be isolated. It is always feared that other countries are taking part in their national affairs.[9] Germany and Finland also want to cooperate more with Russia concerning trade. The presence of Russian companies in the European markets is growing constantly.[10]

Russia has got a lot of mineral resources, conventional and renewable energies, forest and fertile soils. Russian exports consist to nearly 50 percent of natural resources. This means that there is only few processing and only a low added value. Russia tried to develop the country in the industrial sector, but they succeeded only in the oil fields in Siberia and the pipeline infrastructure.[11]

The trade partners can be separated into two major groups: the EU-countries and the GUS- countries. But the EU- states are nearly seeing Russia only as a country exporting energy to them; they want to import oil and gas. The EU-states depend on the Russian oil and gas very much. Russia has become more attractive for these states during the last years due to the increasing prices for energy. Russia exports a greater variety of products into the GUS-states, but also here oil is the most important. In the Russian exports to China, Japan and the USA oil is not playing such a big role because

---

[7] Launer, Ekkehard: page 16

[8] Smith, Alan: *Russia and the world economy. Problems of integration.* New York: Routledge 1993

[9] Fischer, Peter A.: *Quer durch das neue Russland. Reportagen zur russischen Wirtschaft und Gesellschaft.* Zürich: Verlag Neue Zürcher Zeitung 2008: page 78

[10] Ivanenko, Vlad: *Rußlands Platz auf dem Weltmarkt. Exportstruktur und Integrationsoptionen.* In: Ost Europa 57. Jahrgang no.4 (April 2007): page 52-55

[11] Ibid: page 58

there is no pipeline network like into the European countries. Never the less the export into these states is increasing. This shows that Russia tries to explore new markets.[12]

4. Situation of the timber industry in Russia

Scientists estimate that the timber industry brings the Russian economy about 20 billion dollars every year.[13]

But still the Russian timber industry could play a more important role in the economy. In 2004 timber and wood processing only made four percent of the production in Russia. According to some scientists the timber industry could be like a gold mine. 25 percent of the forests of the world are in Russia. "The total area of forests in the Russian federation is 1173, 4 million ha, and the reserves of standing wood exceed 82 billion cubic meters.[14] The annual increase of wood in Russian forests is 932, 2 million cubic meters with an allowable cut of 520 million cubic meters, of which only 22% are currently used. Thus, the potential of the national timber industry is no less than the oil, iron and steel industries." [15] The timber industry could develop to one of the most important industries in Russia.

The regions with a lot of wood are Primorsky, Khabarovsk, and Irkutsk. They belong to South-eastern Siberia and the Far East of Russia. After the era of Gorbachev and his perestroika a lot of wood processing companies were closed. That led to a loss of many jobs, taxes and energy. 1989 more wood was used regionally. So about the half was needed for the usage in their own region. A quarter was used in other regions, and 30 percent was sent to other countries. In that time 20 percent of the timber production was processed timber like sawn wood and plywood. The amount of processed wood decreased a lot. Nowadays the amount is only seven percent. Today the roundwood production (which is only very less processed wood) is growing in the regions with a lot of forestry, but it still has not reached the level of 1985, when it was very high. The sawn

---

[12] Ibid: page 57
[13] http://en.wikipedia.org/wiki/Forestry_in_Russia
[14] http://www.zukunftsregion.org/desktopdefault.aspx/tabid-1889/
[15] http://www.russianforestryreview.com/files/docs/rfr_promo.pdf page 3

wood production reached its climax in 1990 and it is falling constantly. The detail course you can see in Picture 1 and in Picture 2.[16]

During the Soviet era too much wood was harvested. Out of this reason the quality of the forests decreased. Mature conifer forests were replaced by shrubs and deciduous trees. Some experts maintain that the decline in timber harvest shows that the forests could recover from the over logging [17]

5. Problems

A general problem is that today a lot of timber is harvested in a wasteful and destructive way. Especially the Asian markets are interested in large diameter valuable trees. Therefore only the best trees are cut. Because of the lack of processing companies small pieces of wood and branches are left on the grounds. In former times these pieces were used to produce plywood out of it. It is also possible to make woodchips out of them, but there are only some producing companies in Russia today. This increases the risk of wildfires. (See chapter 5.3) The logging of timber in protected rivers causes a lot of damages to plants and animals at the banks.[18]

5.1. Economic problems

Russia wants to support investments into the processing wood industry. It wants to invest at least 300 million Rubble which was about 8, 1 million Euro in 2008. The requirement is that the wood has to be processed on the Russian ground. The first aim is to support the construction of low wood houses because it needs a lot of raw materials. On top of that the government wants to make new streets in the forests and to abandon customs duty on imported machines to process timber. For comparison in

---

[16] http://www.forestsmonitor.org/en/reports/548670/549162
[17] http://www.forestsmonitor.org/en/reports/548670/549162
[18] http://www.forestsmonitor.org/en/reports/548670/549162

Russia are 1, 5 km of streets in the forests per 1 ha of forest, but in Western Europe and in North America there are 10 to 40 km per 1 ha forest.[19] [20]

The lack of streets in the forests holds back the development of the timber industry in Russia.

Since 2006 the customs on round timber are increased constantly to strengthen the regional forest processing. The aim is that the exports of unprocessed woods are not profitable anymore. They are beginning to succeed. The export of round wood decreased in January 2008 in comparison to the month of the year before. The need of wood for furniture, building material and paper can be satisfied only by a half of the domestic wood production, the rest has to be imported, although Russia has 25 percent of forest worldwide.[21] [22] This shows a mismanagement of the Russian industry because Russia exports the world's largest amount of wood (but a huge part of it is unprocessed wood).

Furthermore a big problem is the low quality of timber processing in Russia because many machines are very old, as you can see on Picture 3.[23] [24] Therefore the gain out of the sold timber is quite low.

Another economic problem results from illegal logging. There is a new EU timber legislation which forces timber importers to verify the legality of their products. This regulation becomes effective on March 3rd, 2013. The consequence may be that Russia must not export timber to Europe anymore.[25] Therefore probably the profits will decrease a lot.

---

[19] http://www.holzconsulting.de/aktuell/branchenmeldungen/russlandwillinvestitioneninholzindustriesubv.php

[20] Aström, Sven-Erik: From Tar to Timber. Studies in Northeast European Forest Exploitation and Foreign Trade 1660-1860. Helsinki: Finnish Society of Sciences and Letters 1988: page 125-127

[21] http://www.holzconsulting.de/aktuell/branchenmeldungen/russlandwillinvestitioneninholzindustriesubv.php

[22] Peter, Marcus: Russia and the WTO. Comparative analysis of Russian and WTO law. Baden-Baden: Nomos Verlagsgesellschaft 2004: page 43-44

[23] http://www.holzconsulting.de/aktuell/branchenmeldungen/russlandwillinvestitioneninholzindustriesubv.php

[24] http://www.wirtschaftsblatt.at/home/international/osteuropa/268931/index.do

[25] http://www.iucn.org/about/union/secretariat/offices/europe/?8302/Russia-may-lose-the-EU-timber-market

5.2. Illegal logging

Illegal logging is probably the problem of the Russian timber industry the country has to suffer from mostly. That is because illegal logging leads to many different kinds of problems, like social conflicts, ecological damages and industrial problems.

Illegal logging means that national or international laws are violated at the time of harvesting the wood, at the transportation, at the buying or at the selling. [26]

At the moment nearly 50 percent of the cut wood is logged illegally. The number is that high because there is not much law enforcement because there are not enough supervisors and on top of that it is estimated that the majority of the supervisors are corrupt.[27] The official number of the percentage of illegally logged wood is 10 percent, so the state Russia says that there is less illegal logging then there is actually.[28] NGOs are often more close to reality, so they can estimate the number better and they are saying the real number and they are not lying.

The industry has to suffer at lot because there is a deformation of competition, for every right company there are many disadvantages. There is also a big economic loss; the state has many lost revenues, but also the forest owners and the industry. Illegal logging leads to a decrease of the timber price because the customers are sceptical and cannot trust all timber companies anymore, so with every timber they buy there is the chance that it is logged illegally and so they pay less for it. [29]

The social problems of illegal logging are huge; a bad national economy hurts everyone, because the state has to suffer from financial losses. And the forests are protecting the climate, so everyone has to suffer from polluted air more. The gains of illegal logging are only helping a few people, the persons who violate the law, but the majority has disadvantages, so it is really unjust. The forests are breaking and so their livelihood is gone because the forests are their main source of earnings.[30]

---

[26] http://www.wwf.de/themen-projekte/waelder/waldvernichtung/illegaler-holzeinschlag/
[27] http://www.illegal-logging.info/item_single.php?it_id=2118&it=news
[28] http://www.ens-newswire.com/ens/apr2008/2008-04-10-02.html
[29] http://www.wwf.de/themen-projekte/waelder/waldvernichtung/illegaler-holzeinschlag/
[30] Ibid

We should not forget the ecological problems following illegal logging. Complete forest areas are clear-cut, therefore it is not sustainable. The wildlife gets destroyed. On this destroyed areas they build plantations for justification, but the nutrients of the soil are disappearing very soon, often because they only plant monocultures, so only one type of plant.[31] Sometimes it is even not just a justification, but the reason why the criminals are logging illegally is because they want to use the areas for planting different crops, for example palm oil, but often they are again just having monocultures. Therefore they have to clear new forests quite soon. [32]

All this is even supported by the political non-transparency of the country, the weak governmental structures, the lack of knowledge, and the missing enforcement of the laws. [33]

5.3. Wildfires

But there are also natural disasters, which affect the Russian timber industry. The worst natural disaster for the forests is wildfires.

These wildfires are not only bad for the forestry, but also for the people and the whole country. The health of many people is in danger because of the smoke and the traffic is disturbed because often it is not possible to see over a distance over a hundred meters. These are not problems, which only occur in the very close areas to the forests, but also in the whole country. The wind is the reason why the smoke gets very far away. The environment and the climate also have to suffer from the huge amounts of CO_2 released in the air through these fires. The air pollution can be, in times with many wildfires, ten times higher than normally. Every year some people die because of the fire and many people are hurt. In the year 2010 over 50 people died in Russia and over 500 were hurt.[34] Over 2000 people have lost their homes.[35]

---

[31] Ibid
[32] http://www.nachhaltigkeit.info/artikel/regenwaelder_illegaler_holzeinschlag_illegal_logg_1201.htm
[33] Ibid

[34] http://www.spiegel.de/panorama/0,1518,710250,00.html

The biggest effects are of course on the timber industry. All trees which are burned cannot be used to sell them or process. The reason why wildfires happen are always hot temperatures, the leaves or branches are starting to burn and it is even possible that the peat soil burns. Left braches on the ground increase the danger a lot. Also if there are some regions where nobody cares about the forest the risk of wildfires is higher because there the trees are very close to each other and much combustible material is on the ground. Sometimes there are also people who set the forest on fire for purpose, but in Russia these people are not significant.

5.4. Ecological problems

There are not only ecological problems resulting from illegal logging but there are also many other ecological problems of the timber industry.

Russia has the largest area of old growth forest in the world.[36] The Russian nature protection wants to keep the Russian wilderness as national parks because there are a lot of rare plants and animals, whereas the forestry wants to use the forests and meadows for its interests. Already 1916, one year before the Russian Revolution, two natural reserves with 2810 square kilometres were established. Until 1993 72 natural reserves came in addition. Not even tourism is allowed in these natural reserves, but it is possible in national parks.[37]

The timber industry contributes to destroy the forests. It is especially interested in the stock of woods of the northern conifer forests, especially if the forest can be reached by streets. Since the breakdown of the former Soviet Union it is much easier for foreign companies to buy natural goods for strong western money.[38] The lack of governmental authority facilitates corruption and decreases the protection of the forest.

[35] http://www.csmonitor.com/World/Europe/2010/0808/Russia-wildfires-Thick-toxic-smog-chokes-Moscow-residents
[36] http://www.illegal-logging.info/item_single.php?it_id=1942&it=news
[37] http://www.waldwissen.net/lernen/weltforstwirtschaft/wsl_naturschutz_russland/index_DE
[38] Ibid

There are only few members of the public nature conservation authority to cope with the businessmen. The consequence is the destruction of large landscapes.[39]

The ecological problems got worse due to the technological progress. In former times two strong men with two axes could cut only a few trees on one day. With a chainsaw the number of cut trees increased. Nowadays there are harvesters, full automatically wood harvesting machines, which cut the trees, remove small branches, cut to a given length and put the logs on the side of the street, like you can see on Picture 4 and Picture 5. They are cutting much more trees, without manual work. Only one worker is necessary. [40]

As a lot of small pieces of wood are left on the ground harvesters destroy a lot of nature and increase the danger of wildfires (See chapter 5.3.)

6. Solutions

There are so many problems so we have to solve them. Nobody wants to have a bad situation for ever. Everyone wants to improve the situation. Russia has started solving some problems, but not all of them and it is not always succeeding in the problems it tries to solve. We have to have in mind that not all problems can be solved together because some are in a contradicting conflict. The enhancement of the economy results often in disadvantages for the environment and vice versa.

6.1. Solutions for the economical problems

To develop the economic situation of the forestry sector the infrastructure has to be increased a lot. The government has to continue to build streets, especially in the forests. But we have to take into consideration that the new harvesters and forwarders do not need as good streets as old tractors and other old machines needed because of their caterpillar system. However streets are still needed for the transportation of the logs.

---

[39] Ibid
[40] http://www.waldwissen.net/technik/holzernte/maschinen/bfw_wissen_harvester/index_DE

It is very important to abandon the customs on new valuable machines to process timber to increase the quality of the domestic processed timber. The economy will profit a lot from that because the Asian and European markets are especially interested in high quality timber.[41] [42] The more the wood is processed the higher are the benefits which are gained in Russia.

If Russia is developing the quality of their domestic wood products it will also earn more money at the Russian market because there is a need of high quality products in Russia as well which are imported today.

If the problem of illegal logging will be solved a big economic problem is improved, too, because Russia will still be able to export timber to Europe after March 2013. This results in good prices and enhances the economic situation of the Russian timber industry.

6.2. Solutions for illegal logging

A solution for this significant problem is the building of institutions and the support of forest protection patrols.[43] There have to be gates, so that it is easier for the officials to control. The roads also have to be controlled in a more regular way. Therefore much more supervisors are necessary; at the moment the number of them is way too small, law enforcement is today not possible.

Another solution is an independent certification system. The EU would support such an idea.[44] To realise this system general measures against corruption have to be done, for example a better payment and a stronger control of the officials. But the EU-countries themselves also have to pay attention not to by the illegally logged timber, although it is often cheaper.

---

[41] http://www.forestsmonitor.org/en/reports/548670/549162
[42] Lasch, Ines/ Leymann, Angela: *Der Tanz mit dem russischen Bären. Strategien für langfristigen Erfolg in Russland.* Heidelberg: Redline Wirtschaft, Redline GmbH 2007

[43] http://www.wwf.de/themen-projekte/waelder/waldvernichtung/illegaler-holzeinschlag/
[44] Ibid

In general we can say that clear regulations and strict laws are necessary. There have to be clear rules in which area it is allowed to cut and in which it is forbidden.

But we have to keep in mind that not more legality means automatically more sustainability. Just to legalise the logging in the way many companies are logging today is not helping the environment and the industry.

6.3 Solutions for the wildfires

How can we solve the wildfires? When wildfires are already there, fire-fighter planes are helping a lot. Often other countries are also helping with their fire-fighter planes because sometimes in Russia there are not enough, when there are fires all over the country: around Moscow, in the centre of Russia and in the east. To fight better against the flames the fire-fighter machines have to be modernised because at the moment they are often too old, so often in smaller regions people had to fight against the flames by their own, sometimes even just with their hands.[45]

A solution would also be to employ the 70.000 rangers again, which were dismissed some time ago. They can blow out the fire quicker than it happens now and they can inform the government very quickly.[46]

To prevent wildfires the removal of the small wooden pieces on the ground would help a lot.

Another solution to really prevent many wildfires is a selective falling. Some specific areas have to be clear cut, although environmentalists are often against it because they think too many trees are cut through this way. The advantage of the selective cutting is that is an easy way of preventing wildfires because with enough forest aisles wildfires cannot spread anymore.

---

[45] http://www.spiegel.de/panorama/0,1518,710250,00.html
[46] Ibid

6.4. Solutions for the ecological problems

The ecological situation of the forests can only be improved by regulations. Russia should have clear concepts and ideas about the usage and about the protection of its forests.[47] When reserves are there, you also need persons to protect them; otherwise the law will always be broken. There should be regulations in which areas harvesters are allowed and where they should be forbidden, so the cutting of the trees happens in a controlled way. Furthermore the companies could be obliged by laws to recycle the small pieces of wood and branches. The consequence would be that the timber consumption for example for the production of paper and ply wood would decrease because you can use the small pieces for the production of these. Another effect would be that the ground would be cleaner than today, so the risk of wildfires would decrease, too.

7. Conclusion

All in all we can say that the situation of the Russian timber industry is quite difficult at the moment. The government is not caring very much, they are only passing some weak laws, which are also not enforced enough. Nevertheless the situation can be improved. If the government, NGOs, local companies, and the countries importing timber from Russia, are starting to work together, to cooperate more, to focus the same aim, it is not very unrealistic that there will be quite a big change in the Russian timber industry within the next years. Somehow it would be an advantage for everyone.

The difficulty is that Russia has to invest money, probably more than it wants to invest. This money should be used to develop the infrastructure because so many streets are needed, but also to pay the works enough money so that they are less corrupt and to employ more rangers to react better to wildfires. Generally we can say that the timber has to be processed more in Russia, so the quality of the timber has to increase.

Of course the state Russia has to make the biggest efforts, you can see that for example because it has to make many new regulations and enforce them. With these new

---

[47] http://www.waldwissen.net/lernen/weltforstwirtschaft/wsl_naturschutz_russland/index_DE

regulations the amount of wood, the way of cutting and also the place of cutting should be controlled. The situation can never get perfect because some problems are always contradicting to others, like the selective cutting against the wildfires is sometimes bad for the environment because of these big clear cut areas, or the use of the new machines helps the economy but is at the same time bad for the environment. So Russia has to find the middle, it has to get a balance between all the problems and their solutions. It has to find the best way for improvement trough experts. Compromises are necessary, they are the only solution.

There is such a great potential of the forestry sector in Russia because of it amounts of wood that there will be hope for the timber industry as long as not every tree is cut down, at least with a bit optimism.

Bibliography

Aström, Sven-Erik: *From Tar to Timber. Studies in Northeast European Forest Exploitation and Foreign Trade 1660-1860.* Helsinki: Finnish Society of Sciences and Letters 1988

Fischer, Peter A.: *Quer durch das neue Russland. Reportagen zur russischen Wirtschaft und Gesellschaft.* Zürich: Verlag Neue Zürcher Zeitung 2008

Peter, Marcus: *Russia and the WTO. Comparative analysis of Russian and WTO law.* Baden-Baden: Nomos Verlagsgesellschaft 2004

Smith, Alan: *Russia and the world economy. Problems of integration.* New York: Routledge 1993

Lasch, Ines/ Leymann, Angela: *Der Tanz mit dem russischen Bären. Strategien für langfristigen Erfolg in Russland.* Heidelberg: Redline Wirtschaft, Redline GmbH 2007

Launer, Ekkehard: *Zum Beispiel Holz. Hört mit der Zerstörung der Wälder auf, oder wir sind gezwungen, sie zu verteidigen.* Göttingen: Lamuv Verlag: 1989

Holzberger, Rudi / Fesseler, Ernst: *Der Wald. Zwischen Wildnis und Monokultur.* Ravensburg: Buchverlag Otto Maier 1989

Köpf, Ernst Ulrich: *Forstpolitik.* Stuttgart: Verlag Eugen Ulmer 2002

Zundel, Rolf: *Einführung in die Forstwirtschaft.* Stuttgart: Verlag Eugen Ulmer 1990

Ivanenko, Vlad: *Rußlands Platz auf dem Weltmarkt. Exportstruktur und Integrationsoptionen.* In: Ost Europa 57. Jahrgang no.4 (April 2007)

http://www.spiegel.de/panorama/0,1518,710250,00.html 20.05.2012

http://www.waldwissen.net/technik/holzernte/maschinen/bfw_wissen_harvester/index_D E 21.05.2012

http://www.waldwissen.net/lernen/weltforstwirtschaft/wsl_naturschutz_russland/index_D E 20.05.2012

http://www.holzconsulting.de/aktuell/branchenmeldungen/russlandwillinvestitioneninholzi
ndustriesubv.php 29.04.2012

http://www.wwf.de/themen-projekte/waelder/waldvernichtung/illegaler-holzeinschlag/
18.05.2012

http://en.wikipedia.org/wiki/Forestry_in_Russia 05.05.2012

http://www.russianforestryreview.com/files/docs/rfr_promo.pdf 12.05.2012

http://www.iucn.org/about/union/secretariat/offices/europe/?8302/Russia-may-lose-the-
EU-timber-market 20.05.2012

http://www.lwf.bayern.de/waldbewirtschaftung/betriebswirtschaft-
forsttechnik/forsttechnik/holzeinschlag/38911/index.php 13.05.2012

http://www.csmonitor.com/World/Europe/2010/0808/Russia-wildfires-Thick-toxic-smog-
chokes-Moscow-residents 19.05.2012

http://www.forestsmonitor.org/en/reports/548670/549162 29.04.2012

http://www.illegal-logging.info/item_single.php?it_id=1942&it=news 02.01.2012

http://www.borderwatch.com.au/news/local/news/general/timber-festival-
boom/2502751.aspx 20.05.2012 22.05.2012

http://www.zukunftsregion.org/desktopdefault.aspx/tabid-1889/ 20.05.2012

http://www.wirtschaftsblatt.at/home/international/osteuropa/268931/index.do 18.05.2012

http://www.nachhaltigkeit.info/artikel/regenwaelder_illegaler_holzeinschlag_illegal_logg_
1201.htm 22.05.2012

http://www.ens-newswire.com/ens/apr2008/2008-04-10-02.html 06.02.2012

http://www.illegal-logging.info/item_single.php?it_id=2118&it=news 13.05.2012

Appendix

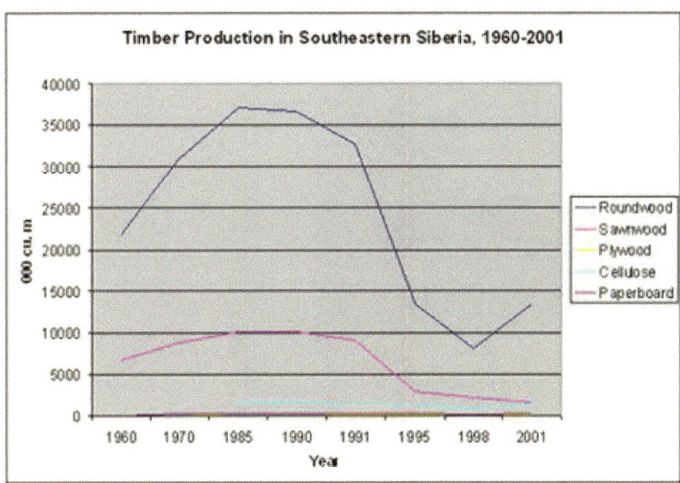

Picture 1: Timber Production in South-eastern Siberia 1960-2001

http://www.forestsmonitor.org/en/reports/548670/549162 Source: Economic Research Institute, Far Eastern Branch of Russian Academy of Sciences

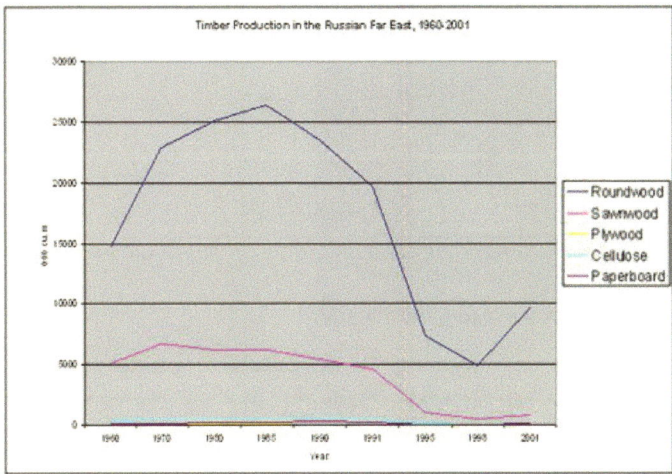

Picture 2: Timber Production in the Russian Far East, 1960-2001

http://www.forestsmonitor.org/en/reports/548670/549162 Source: Economic Research Institute, Far Eastern Branch of Russian Academy of Sciences

Picture 3: Old tractor in Russia

http://www.borderwatch.com.au/news/local/news/general/timber-festival-boom/2502751.aspx

Picture 4: A working harvester

http://www.lwf.bayern.de/waldbewirtschaftung/betriebswirtschaft-
forsttechnik/forsttechnik/holzeinschlag/38911/index.php

Picture 5: A cutting harvester

http://www.lwf.bayern.de/waldbewirtschaftung/betriebswirtschaft-
forsttechnik/forsttechnik/holzeinschlag/38911/index.php